# SPIRITUAL
## REFLECTIONS
### WITH
### UNVEILED
## FACE

# SPIRITUAL
## REFLECTIONS
## WITH
## UNVEILED
## FACE

A 40-DAY JOURNEY OF PRAYERS, REFLECTIONS AND DEVOTIONS

**AUDREY J. MURRELL, PH.D.**

XULON PRESS

Xulon Press
2301 Lucien Way #415
Maitland, FL 32751
407.339.4217
www.xulonpress.com

© 2022 by Audrey J. Murrell, Ph.D.

All rights reserved solely by the author. The author guarantees all contents are original and do not infringe upon the legal rights of any other person or work. No part of this book may be reproduced in any form without the permission of the author.

Due to the changing nature of the Internet, if there are any web addresses, links, or URLs included in this manuscript, these may have been altered and may no longer be accessible. The views and opinions shared in this book belong solely to the author and do not necessarily reflect those of the publisher. The publisher therefore disclaims responsibility for the views or opinions expressed within the work.

Unless otherwise indicated, Scripture quotations taken from the Holy Bible, New International Version (NIV). Copyright © 1973, 1978, 1984, 2011 by Biblica, Inc.™. Used by permission. All rights reserved.

Paperback ISBN-13: 978-1-66285-012-7
Ebook ISBN-13: 978-1-66285-199-5

*This book is dedicated to the memory of Beverly Jean Hall-Murrell, whose life was pure poetry in words, in deeds, and always, in love.*

# Table of Contents

| Reflection | Scripture Reading | Page |
|---|---|---|
| Dear Hope | Hebrews 6:19 | 2 |
| The Author of All Possibilities | Matthew 19:26 | 4 |
| Lean On | Proverbs 3:5-6 | 6 |
| Enduring Mercies | Psalm 107:1 | 8 |
| Confidence | Philippians 1:6 | 10 |
| Selah | Matthew 11:28 | 12 |
| Never Changing | Hebrews 13:8 | 14 |
| Treasuring Mercy | Psalm 40:11 | 16 |
| No Rest for the Weary | Isaiah 40:31 | 18 |
| In His Hands | Psalm 33:10-11 | 20 |
| Masks | Proverbs 26:24-26 | 22 |
| Shine Anyway | Matthew 5:14-16 | 24 |
| God Is Able | Ephesians 3:20 | 26 |
| Soak in God | Psalm 5:11-12 | 28 |
| By Grace | Ephesians 2:8-9 | 30 |
| Perseverance | James 1:4 | 32 |
| Not the Final Say | Hebrews 12:1-3 | 34 |
| He Told You So | John 15:18-19 | 36 |

| | | |
|---|---|---|
| His Love Endures | Psalm 136:1-3 | 38 |
| Custom-Made | Jeremiah 29:11 | 40 |
| You Go, Girl! | Psalm 139:13-14 | 42 |
| Give Thanks | Thessalonians 5:16-18 | 44 |
| Divine Openings | Matthew 7:7-8 | 46 |
| God Is the Same | Hebrews 13:8 | 48 |
| Kingdom Math | Luke 6:38 | 50 |
| What a Difference a Day Makes | Lamentations 3:22-23 | 52 |
| The "T" Word | Psalm 20:7 | 54 |
| Doing Good | Galatians 6:9 | 56 |
| God's Favor | Psalm 90:17 | 58 |
| Hope Won't Disappoint | Romans 5:5 | 60 |
| To God | Jude 24-25 | 62 |
| All Things | Romans 8:28 | 64 |
| Just Because | Psalm 83:18 | 66 |
| Launch Out | Luke 5:4 | 68 |
| A New Thing | Isaiah 43:18-19 | 70 |
| My Heart's Desire | Psalm 51:10 | 72 |
| Daily Loveliness | Philippians 4:8 | 74 |
| Highest Praise | Psalm 145:1-3 | 76 |
| His Spirit | 2 Timothy 1:7 | 78 |
| Rejoice Always | Philippians 4:4-7 | 80 |

# From the Author

Before the pandemic, I used to write for pleasure, inspiration, and reflection a lot. Then it stopped. The busyness of the day, work, personal responsibilities, and, perhaps, a cluttered life that seemed to match my cluttered home was both a distraction and an obstacle. But during the COVID-19 pandemic, the anxiety, fear, and uncertainty, coupled with the social distancing and social isolation, moved me to read, write, and reflect much more than I had done in the past few years. I found that I really missed it. And so, I kept writing. Throughout the year, I would go back and re-read some of these spiritual reflections to remember the journey, recall the lessons learned, and remind myself that God was always with me, directing my path and covering me each step of the way. This journey is beautifully captured by the apostle Paul's words in 2 Corinthians 3:12-18, who described believers' prayers and petitions as turning to God *"with unveiled faces."* What a powerful image! I hope that these writings inspire you to create your own spiritual reflections and to be true, honest, open, weary, troubled, angry, lonely, fearful, and, most of all, *authentic* before God. And because of the finished work of the cross, we each can go to God with an unveiled face. My sincere prayer is that these reflections can become your personal reminder that no matter what we navigate through in our lives, God is always with us as He promised (Deut.

31:6). Thank you for being an extended part of my spiritual journey. I hope that what you read blesses you, revives you, and inspires you as much as it has—and still does—for me. Remember to keep thanking God for the amazing things that He does for us and through us—if we only take the time to stop, pray, and reflect with an unveiled face...

Grace and Peace,
**Audrey**

# "With Unveiled Faces"

*But whenever anyone turns to the Lord, the veil is taken away. Now the Lord is the Spirit, and where the Spirit of the Lord is, there is freedom. And we all, who with unveiled faces contemplate the Lord's glory, are being transformed into His image with ever-increasing glory, which comes from the Lord, who is the Spirit.*

2 Corinthians 3:16-18 (NIV)

# A Special Note: The Significance of the Number "40"

This book contains forty spiritual reflections with Scripture as both a foundation and an inspiration. While I am not a follower of numerology (the study or belief in the divine or mystical value of the letters in words, names, ideas, events, or outcomes that number forty[1]), the number forty does have significance throughout Scripture. Some suggest that the number forty signals periods of "testing, trials and triumph."[2] But forty could also be seen as the number signaling "journey," as was the case for Moses during his forty days and forty nights on Mount Sinai (Deut. 9:18) or the forty years that the Israelites wandered in the desert on their way to the promised land (Deut. 8:2-5) or the forty days and forty nights that Jesus Himself was tempted and tested in the wilderness (Matt. 4:2). The number forty also shapes the Christian season of Lent, which is observed each year starting on Ash Wednesday and ending on Resurrection Sunday. Many Christian believers use this Lenten period as a time to reflect on the powerful gift of salvation given to us by the death and resurrection of Jesus Christ. Whatever season you find yourself in as you read this, I hope these forty spiritual reflections and Scripture readings will support and encourage you to record your own personal journey toward a deeper relationship with the One who represents the ultimate destination of our life's journey—*Jesus Christ*.

---

[1] https://www.merriam-webster.com/dictionary/numerology

[2] https://www.womanofnoblecharacter.com/40-in-the-bible/

# A Brief Overview of the Book

This book is organized into three (3) parts:

1. **Spiritual Reflections** – These are my own personal reflections, inspirations, ruminations, thoughts, struggles, angers, pains, frustrations, regrets, and revelations. Use these to help stimulate your own thinking and reflections. I've provided space for you to record your own spiritual reflections along this next phase of the journey.

2. **Scripture Reading** – Included is a passage of Scripture that helps me to ground these reflections in the Word of God as recorded in the Bible. This is important to help us remember that for everything we go through, every road we travel, every success or failure can be found in and understood through the Word of God. I encourage you to use whatever version of the Bible is most inspiring for you, read each scripture referenced, and then add your own reflections and hand-picked scriptures to the ones included here. This makes each spiritual reflection based on the Word of God personal to you, your needs, your circumstances, and your own journey.

3. **Personal Reflections, Prayers, Praises, and Petitions** – There is space for you to add your own

reflections and requests and space for you to record your laments (cries), praises, and prayers. These can be for yourself or on behalf of someone else who you feel a need to go to God for. It has helped me to write these down and revisit them from time to time so I may see the journey that God and I have taken together—a journey that has helped me to *"Always be prepared to give an answer to everyone who asks you to give the reason for the hope that you have. But do this with gentleness and respect"* (1 Peter 3:15, NIV).

# Spiritual Reflections

# Dear Hope

Dear hope – please come!
Show yourself to me.
Come without delay.
I feel you less in these days.
When trouble seems near,
You feel far away.

More fear versus more faith?
Less hope versus more hope?

More trouble versus more prayer?
Less hope versus more hope?

More trials versus more study?
Less hope versus more hope?

But God gives hope in abundance
To prosper and not to harm—
For my future.
For my good.

Dear hope – you are always with me.
Help me to believe.
Help me to choose each day

Hope.

***Scripture Reading: Hebrews 6:19***

# Personal Reflections

What does hope as an "anchor for the soul" mean to you during this point or season in your life?

_____

_____

_____

_____

_____

_____

_____

What are your own "poetic reflections" and/or prayers to God about "hope"?

_____

_____

_____

_____

_____

_____

_____

_____

# The Author of All Possibilities

I need not be discouraged.
I should not be dismayed.
I need not be so weary.
I should not lose hope.
I need not give up trying.
I should not quit or run.
I need not think I failed.
I should not call myself worthless.

But God Who is the Author.
But God Who is the Finisher.
But God Who is where hope and possibilities dwell.

I need to look at Him for hope.
I should fix my eyes on Him.
I need to remember all He has done.
I should dwell on Him and not my troubles.
I need to recall His promises.
I should realize that I'm not alone.
I need to recite His Word daily.
I should keep my heart on the possibilities of God.

***Scripture Reading: Matthew 19:26***

# Personal Reflections

What parts of your life do you see as possible versus impossible?

_____

_____

_____

_____

_____

_____

_____

What are your own "poetic reflections" and/or prayers to God about possibilities?

_____

_____

_____

_____

_____

_____

_____

_____

# Lean On

What do you lean on
When the world doesn't make sense?

What do you lean on
When trouble comes and stays?

What do you lean on
When so-called friends walk away?

What do you lean on
When problems and haters stick like glue?

What do you lean on
Through sadness, grief, and loss?

What do you lean on
When your plans fail and you feel lost?

What do you lean on
When you are tired and weary in spirit?

What do you lean on?
The One Who understands, forgives, protects, heals, and directs your path.

What do you lean on?
The truth found in the Word of God.

***Scripture Reading: Proverbs 3:5-6***

# Personal Reflections

Who or what do you trust and lean on in times of trouble or struggle?

_____

_____

_____

_____

_____

_____

_____

What are your own "poetic reflections" and/or prayers to God about trusting and leaning on Him?

_____

_____

_____

_____

_____

_____

_____

# Enduring Mercies

Mercies are the compassion we receive from You.

Mercies are the journey we take together along life's road.

Mercies are new and fresh every day.

Mercies are the gifts You give when I want to quit.

Mercies are the compassionate embrace when sorrow overwhelms me.

Your mercies overflow.
Your mercies are faithful.
Your mercies are steadfast.
Your mercies never fail.
Your mercies are abundant.

I give thanks for Your mercies in times of trouble and strife.

I give thanks for Your steadfast love when I want to give up.

I give thanks for Your faithful mercies as I am tossed about by trouble.

I give thanks for Your endurance when I am weary in spirit.

I give thanks for Your loving mercies that always endure.

***Scripture Reading: Psalm 107:1***

# Personal Reflections

What does "enduring mercies" mean to you, and how have you experienced that in your life?

_____

_____

_____

_____

_____

_____

_____

What are your own "poetic reflections" and/or prayers to God for enduring mercies?

_____

_____

_____

_____

_____

_____

_____

_____

# Confidence

Assurance.
Boldness.
Certainty.
Conviction.
Belief.
Trust.
Inner Knowledge.
Clear-headed.
Focused.
Faith.

Quite a list?
Impossible?
Improbable?
Aspirational?
Inspirational?

Ask for assurance.
Seek greater confidence.
Request inner knowledge.
Knock on the door of boldness.

It will be opened for you!
You have full access!
Trust and believe!
By faith!
With confidence!

***Scripture Reading: Philippians 1:6***

# Personal Reflections

In what or whom do you put your confidence in during both good times and bad times?

_____

_____

_____

_____

_____

_____

_____

What are your own "poetic reflections" and/or prayers to God related to having more confidence?

_____

_____

_____

_____

_____

_____

_____

_____

# Selah

Rest
Revival
Renewal
Rejuvenation

*SELAH*

Running
Running
More Running
Still Running

*SELAH*

Emptied
Fatigued
Lacking
Spent

*SELAH*

Finished
Used
Emptied
Exhausted

*SELAH*

Pause
Wait
Listen
Receive

*SELAH*

**Scripture Reading: Matthew 11:28**

# Personal Reflections

What do you do that brings you rest and renewal and rejuvenates you?

_____

_____

_____

_____

_____

_____

_____

What are your own "poetic reflections" and/or prayers to God as you seek rest?

_____

_____

_____

_____

_____

_____

_____

_____

# Never Changing

People,
You think you know them
But they have many, many faces.

Loyalty faces.
Friendship faces.
Familiar faces.
Deceitful faces.
Betrayal faces.
Jealousy faces.

False, fake, phony, untrue faces.

How do you survive when you can't recognize the faces staring back at you?

Look to God.

He is the same

Yesterday,

Today,

Tomorrow,

Next week,

Next year,

Forever.

His face will never change.

***Scripture Reading: Hebrews 13:8***

# Personal Reflections

What experiences do you have with God being "the same" yesterday, today, and tomorrow?

_____

_____

_____

_____

_____

_____

_____

What are your own "poetic reflections" and/or prayers to remind you of specific times in your life when you learned that God will never change?

_____

_____

_____

_____

_____

_____

_____

# Treasuring Mercy

God's loving kindness.
Great is God's mercy.
God's covenant with His believers.
Compassion given.
Forgiveness not earned.

Mercy endures.

Mercy is everlasting.

Mercy is unmerited.

Mercy is freely given.

Mercy is a gift.

Mercy is a promise.

Mercy is overflowing.

Mercy is love.

Let me feel mercy each day—
To recognize it and give thanks,
To call it out with my praise,
To keep it in my heart for bad days,
To remember it when faced with hate,
To be thankful for such an amazing gift.

Let me treasure mercy
Each and every day.

***Scripture Reading: Psalm 40:11***

# Personal Reflections

What does mercy mean to you, and how have you received or witnessed mercy during your life?

_____

_____

_____

_____

_____

_____

_____

What are your own "poetic reflections" and/or prayers to God about your need for His mercy?

_____

_____

_____

_____

_____

_____

_____

# No Rest for the Weary

*No rest for the weary.*
What an odd saying!
Rest is what the weary need—
What they require,
What will sustain them,
What will refuel them,
What God requires of them.

Rest.

Renewal.

Repair.

Restore.

Rethink.

Retool.

Replenish.

Revive.

That peace that surpasses all understanding comes from rest.
You only hear still waters during times of rest.
God's voice becomes clearer in a season of rest.
Yes, rest for the weary.

Rest.

**Scripture Reading: Isaiah 40:31**

# Personal Reflections

When are times you have felt weary, and where or who do you turn to?

_____

_____

_____

_____

_____

_____

_____

What are your own "poetic reflections" and/or prayers to God to sustain your strength?

_____

_____

_____

_____

_____

_____

_____

# In His Hands

The lists.
The ideas.
The meetings.
The visions.
The aspirations.
The hopes.
The dreams.
The desires.

But …

The obstacles.
The resistance.
The failures.
The missteps.
The errors.
The haters.
The unbelievers.
The stonewallers.
The enemies.

But …

He has a plan.
He intends for me to prosper.
He gives me hope.
His plans are no harm for me.
His plans are for my future.
His plans are made just for me.

But …

The plans for me are in His hands!

***Scripture Reading: Psalm 33:10-11***

# Personal Reflections

What plans do you have that you have trusted into God's hands? In what specific ways can you ask God for help? What outcomes does your heart most desire?

_____

_____

_____

_____

_____

_____

_____

What are your own "poetic reflections" and/or prayers to God about your hopes, dreams, and plans?

_____

_____

_____

_____

_____

_____

_____

# Masks

The masks we wear—
Out of fear,
Out of hidden desires,
Out of false intents,
Out of evil roots.
It is hard to recognize what is behind the mask.
It is hard to see what is really underneath.
It is impossible to know the real person.
It is challenging to connect or relate.
It is pointless to cultivate relationships.

Some masks cause pain.
Some masks cause chaos.
Some masks manipulate circumstances.
Some masks hide evil intentions.
Some masks do endless harm.

Help me to see past the masks.
Help me to discern when faces are hidden.
Help me to see past masked actions.
Help me to detect truth from lies.
Help me to see real relationships.

Beyond the masks we wear.

***Scripture Reading: Proverbs 26:24-26***

# Personal Reflections

When have you been impacted by the masks that others wear or their false intents?

_____

_____

_____

_____

_____

_____

_____

What are your own "poetic reflections" and/or prayers to God to help you with the pain caused by false intents and masks that others wear?

_____

_____

_____

_____

_____

_____

_____

# Shine Anyway

Seems hard to shine when darkness is all around—
Shine anyway.

Seems impossible to shine when hate persists—
Shine anyway.

Seems unreachable to shine when the bar keeps moving—
Shine anyway.

Seems unlikely to shine when others cheat to win—
Shine anyway.

Why shine?
For what purpose?
What does it matter?
Who cares?

Shine anyway.

When it feels hopeless.
When it seems unbearable.
When it looks unwinnable.
When it appears that all has been lost.

Shine anyway.

Let them know you are here.
Light a path for others to see and to follow.
Let them see God's glory will prevail.
Light a path for others to succeed.

Shine anyway.

***Scripture Reading: Matthew 5:14-16***

# Personal Reflections

In what ways do you either hide your strengths, accomplishments, or positive attributes or in what ways do you let them "shine" for others to see?

_____

_____

_____

_____

_____

_____

_____

What are your own "poetic reflections" and/or prayers to God to strengthen you so that you may shine?

_____

_____

_____

_____

_____

_____

_____

_____

# God Is Able

When I feel powerless,
God is able.

When it looks unreachable,
God is able.

When I think it's unrealizable,
God is able.

When I think it's unachievable,
God is able.

When I believe it's unrealistic,
God is able.

When I think it's over and done,
God is able.

When I think the battle is lost,
God is able.

When I feel all alone,
God is able.

When I think friends are few,
God is able.

When I think hope is lost,
God is able.

When I think that I'm not enough,
God is able.

God is able!

**Scripture Reading: Ephesians 3:20**

# Personal Reflections

When have you felt powerless during your life, and how have you coped or adjusted?

_____

_____

_____

_____

_____

_____

_____

What are your own "poetic reflections" and/or prayers to God to remind you during times of struggle that He is able?

_____

_____

_____

_____

_____

_____

_____

# Soak in God

Soak it in.
Saturate yourself.
Breathe it all in.
Breathe deeply.
Let the sweetness fill the air within your lungs.
Let it wrap you up in joy.

Soak it in.
Make time stop.
Pause and look around.
Breathe and look up.
Be aware of all that surrounds you.

Soak in peace.

Soak in joy.

Soak in love.

Soak in goodness.

Soak in restoration.

Soak in holiness.

Soak in fellowship.

Soak in compassion.

Soak in salvation.

Soak in revelation.

Soak in truth.

Soak in God.

**Scripture Reading: Psalm 5:11-12**

# Personal Reflections

During challenging times, where do you go to seek refuge or relief?

_____

_____

_____

_____

_____

_____

_____


What are your own "poetic reflections" and/or prayers to remind you to soak in God during challenging times?

_____

_____

_____

_____

_____

_____

_____

# By Grace

By grace I have received.

Salvation.
Redemption.
Reconciliation.
Everlasting life.

Forgiveness.
An eternal home.
The Comforter.
An Intercessor.

A Father.
A Protector.
A Friend.
A Redeemer.

Beauty for ashes.
Protection.
Calling.
More grace.

Insights.
Discernment.
Revelation.
Spiritual growth.

Love.
New mercies.
Faith.
A reason to shout and praise.

By grace, I have received

Everything.

***Scripture Reading: Ephesians 2:8-9***

# Personal Reflections

What does the word *grace* mean to you, and when have you experienced God's grace in your life?

_____

_____

_____

_____

_____

_____

_____

What are your own "poetic reflections" and/or prayers to God as a reminder that grace is given freely to you?

_____

_____

_____

_____

_____

_____

_____

_____

# Perseverance

Perseverance
Must
Finish
Its work.

For your growth.
For your maturity.

Then you will not lack.
Then you will have wisdom.

To give you strength.
To give you insight.

So your faith increases.
So your knowledge grows.

And you will receive a crown.
And you will not miss the mark.

Perseverance
Must
Finish
Its work.

Count it as blessings.
Count it as joy.
Count it as gain.
Count it as love.

***Scripture Reading: James 1:4***

# Personal Reflections

What does it mean to you that perseverance "must finish its work" so that you will be complete?

_____

_____

_____

_____

_____

_____

_____


What are your own "poetic reflections" and/or prayers to God so that you can persevere during challenging times?

_____

_____

_____

_____

_____

_____

_____

# Not the Final Say

Whose report will I believe?
Whose words will I acknowledge?
Whose labels will I accept?
Whose judgement will I receive?

What lies will I take in?
What attacks will I fear?
What name will I be called?
What falsehoods will I confess?

When will justice come?
When will apologies be heard?
When will promises be kept?
When will things work for the good?

Why do evildoers win?
Why do liars succeed?
Why do haters celebrate?
Why do accusers prosper?

Whose?
What?
When?
Why?

Nevertheless – many questions.
Nevertheless – only one answer.
God.
Yesterday.
Today.
Tomorrow.
Forever.
Victorious.

***Scripture Reading: Hebrews 12:1-3***

# Personal Reflections

When have the judgements or opinions of others hindered you or weighed you down?

_____

_____

_____

_____

_____

_____

What are your own "poetic reflections" and/or prayers to God to remind you to let go of the weight of others' opinions and judgements?

_____

_____

_____

_____

_____

_____

_____

# He Told You So

He told you so.

He told you they would come.
The resistance.
The weapons.
The challenges.
The trials.
The dangers both seen and unseen.

He told you so.

He told you they would come.
The enemies.
The haters.
The liars.
The scoffers.
The unjust rulers of this world.

He told you so.

He told you He would.
Be in the fire with you.
Be by your side always.
Be there to ensure the waters don't overtake you.
Be there so that formed weapons don't prosper.
Be there to give you hope and a future.

He told you so.

***Scripture Reading: John 15:18-19***

# Personal Reflections

How has the warning (that weapons would form against you) God provided to us given you a sense of comfort during times of trouble?

_____

_____

_____

_____

_____

_____

_____

What are your own "poetic reflections" and/or prayers to God on being reminded of what He has told us?

_____

_____

_____

_____

_____

_____

_____

# His Love Endures

A love that responds.
Meeting your hidden needs.
Unexpected favor.
Unmerited kindness.
Unwarranted forgiveness.

Beyond human love.
Strong in forbearance.
Compassion that's never ending.
Kindness that won't run out.

Relief of pain or suffering.
Help when not requested but needed.
Extended hand even to haters.
Use of justice to judge your actions.

A second chance.
Another shot.
A do-over.
An unrequested free pass.

God's mercy.

God's grace.

God's love.

From everlasting
To everlasting.

A love that endures.

***Scripture Reading: Psalm 136:1-3***

# Personal Reflections

What are some of the experiences, relationships, victories, or other things that you give thanks to God for?

_____

_____

_____

_____

_____

_____

_____

What are your own "poetic reflections" and/or prayers to God for His enduring love?

_____

_____

_____

_____

_____

_____

_____

_____

# Custom-Made

God has special plans for me.
He knows them full well.
He designed them just for me.
They are custom-made from God.

God has remarkable plans for me.
He plans for me to prosper.
He designed plans for my good.
They are custom-made from God.

God has amazing plans for me.
He expects to shield me from harm.
He designed protection for my benefit.
They are custom-made from God.

God has wonderful plans for me.
He created them with hope in my future.
He wrapped them in love.
They are custom-made from God.

God has incredible plans for me.
To prosper.
To hope.
To succeed.
To share.
To love.
To believe.
They are custom-made from God.

For me.

***Scripture Reading: Jeremiah 29:11***

# Personal Reflections

What does it mean to you that God has a plan for you and that plan is for you to prosper?

_____

_____

_____

_____

_____

_____

_____

What are your own "poetic reflections" and/or prayers to God on trusting His plan for you?

_____

_____

_____

_____

_____

_____

_____

_____

# YOU GO, GIRL!

When others belittle you,
Tell you what you ain't,
Call you out your name,

Tell yourself – you go, girl!

When they change the rules,
Move the finish line,
Accuse you of cheating or lying,

Tell yourself – YOU go, girl!

When they talk about your looks,
Your hair, your skin, or your body type,
Compare you to an animal or call you a female dog,

Tell yourself – YOU GO, girl!

When they say you can't make it,
Discourage you from certain pathways,
Make you think you can't perform, can't lead, can't create change in this world,

Tell yourself – YOU GO, GIRL!

YOU GO, GIRL!!!

***Scripture Reading: Psalm 139:13-14***

# Personal Reflections

When have you felt "wonderfully made," and when have you felt negative about yourself because of the criticism of others?

_____

_____

_____

_____

_____

_____

_____

What are your own "poetic reflections" and/or prayers to God to sustain a positive view of yourself as His wonderful creation?

_____

_____

_____

_____

_____

_____

_____

# Give Thanks

Give thanks
With a grateful heart.

Give thanks,
Expecting nothing in return.

Give thanks
For enduring mercies.

Give thanks
For unmerited favor.

Give thanks
For the finished work of the cross.

Give thanks
For sacrificial love.

Give thanks
For being called.

Give thanks
For the indwelling Spirit.

Give thanks
For protection from unseen dangers.

Give thanks.

For every day,
For every step,
For every hug,
For every smile,
For every joy,
For every sorrow,
For every breath,

Give thanks.

***Scripture Reading: 1 Thessalonians 5:16-18***

# Personal Reflections

How have you struggled to be joyful and rejoice in all situations? What has helped you remain thankful and grateful during challenging times or situations?

_____

_____

_____

_____

_____

_____

_____

What are your own "poetic reflections" and/or prayers to God on being thankful in all circumstances?

_____

_____

_____

_____

_____

_____

_____

# Divine Openings

Ask.

Seek.

Knock.

Open.

Openings from God are a gift,
A blessing like no other.
One that nobody can take away.
One you must receive with joy.

Ask.

Seek.

Knock.

Open.

Openings from God are custom-made,
Based on the deepest desires of the heart.
A reflection of the past and the future yet to come.
A love-wrapped gift from our heavenly Father.

Ask.

Seek.

Knock.

Open.

Praise His holy name.
Give God thanks.
Let gratitude fill your heart.
Appreciate divine openings.

***Scripture Reading: Matthew 7:7-8***

# Personal Reflections

What have you asked God for with confidence that you will receive it?

_____

_____

_____

_____

_____

_____

_____

What are your own "poetic reflections" and/or prayers to God as you ask, seek, and wait on His provision?

_____

_____

_____

_____

_____

_____

_____

# God Is the Same

Winds may increase or become silent.
Seasons can come and go.
Years go by faster and faster.
But God is the same.

Fads fade quickly.
What is in soon becomes out.
Trends change into something old-school.
But God is the same.

Enemies abound but soon fail.
Plans succeed but sometimes don't.
Pathways, journeys, and trips can detour.
But God is the same.

What is old is somehow new.
What is new quickly becomes old.
What *is* can become what is forgotten.
But God is the same.

Yesterday.
Today.
Tomorrow.
Forever.

God is the same.

**Scripture Reading: Hebrews 13:8**

# Personal Reflections

How have you experienced God being consistent or reliable in your life? What specific examples or situations can you recall?

_____

_____

_____

_____

_____

_____

_____

What are your own "poetic reflections" and/or prayers to God to trust Him even during times of uncertainty?

_____

_____

_____

_____

_____

_____

_____

# Kingdom Math

Multiplied.

Increased.

Manifold.

Enlarged.

Multiplied.
Producing abundance.
Enlarging territory.

Increased.
Adding to what is.
Causing overflow.

Manifold.
Creating more and more.
Generating many and varied.

Enlarged.
Making what is to be greater.
Expanding a little into much.

Multiplied.

Increased.

Manifold.

Enlarged.

*Scripture Reading: Luke 6:38*

# Personal Reflections

How have you seen the impact of your own "good measure" throughout your life?

_____

_____

_____

_____

_____

_____

_____

What are your own "poetic reflections" and/or prayers to God to value your own "good measure," and how can it multiply?

_____

_____

_____

_____

_____

_____

_____

_____

# What a Difference a Day Makes

Sun follows rain.
Trouble doesn't last always.
Joy comes in the morning.

What a difference a day makes.

Anger subsides.
Hurt will heal.
Forgiveness is given by choice.

What a difference a day makes.

Worry bears no fruit.
Enemies aren't worth the effort.
All things work for our good.

What a difference a day makes.

The joy of the Lord is eternal.
God who never slumbers nor sleeps.
His mercies are new each morning.

What a difference a day makes.

***Scripture Reading: Lamentations 3:22-23***

# Personal Reflections

How have you experienced God's compassion and His faithfulness?

_____
_____
_____
_____
_____
_____
_____

What are your own "poetic reflections" and/or prayers to God to remember His compassion during hard times?

_____
_____
_____
_____
_____
_____
_____

# The "T" Word

Trust in God.
Not in chariots.
Not in horses.
Not in people.
Trust in God.

Lean on Him.
Not your understanding.
Not your vision.
Not your expectations.

Acknowledge Him.
Not your enemies.
Not your haters.
Not your deeds.

For direction shall come.
For knowledge will increase.
For wisdom is going to take root.
For faith will increase.

In all your ways.
Trust in God.
Not in chariots.
Not in horses.
Not in people.

Put your trust in God.

***Scripture Reading: Psalm 20:7***

# Personal Reflections

What are some of the barriers or obstacles that you experience in being able to trust God?

_____

_____

_____

_____

_____

_____

_____

What are your own "poetic reflections" and/or prayers to God to help increase your level of trust?

_____

_____

_____

_____

_____

_____

_____

# Doing Good

Do good.
Even when no one thanks you.

Do good.
Even when they attack you.

Do good.
Even when no one is watching.

Do good.
Even when others are jealous.

Do good.
Even when things don't make sense.

Do good.
Even when it looks like you failed.

Do good.
Even when you're sad and lonely.

Do good.
Even if nothing is gained.

Do good.
Even when you are afraid.

Do good.
In season and out of season.

Do good.
Until you hear, "Well done!"

***Scripture Reading: Galatians 6:9***

# Personal Reflections

What keeps you going as you are trying to "do good" in the world around us?

_____

_____

_____

_____

_____

_____

_____

What are your own "poetic reflections" and/or prayers to God to help you focus on doing good for others around you, regardless of the outcomes or their response?

_____

_____

_____

_____

_____

_____

_____

# God's Favor

God's favor

Is amazing.
Can be overwhelming.
Catches you by surprise.
Is abundant, overflowing, and complete.

God's favor

Is love.
Cannot be taken for granted.
Should never be confused with luck.
Is evidence of His grace and mercy.

God's favor

Is timely.
Can be unexpected blessings.
Will knock you off of your feet.
Is the calm in the midst of life's storms.

God's favor

Is endless.
Can't ever be exhausted or depleted.
Will never be earned or repaid.
Is the gift we receive by faith.

God's favor.

**Scripture Reading: Psalm 90:17**

# Personal Reflections

What does the idea of "God's favor" mean to you, and how have you experienced it in your life?

_____

_____

_____

_____

_____

_____

_____

What are your own "poetic reflections" and/or prayers to God about seeing how His favor is present in your life each day?

_____

_____

_____

_____

_____

_____

_____

_____

# Hope Won't Disappoint

Problems arise.
People stumble.
Plans fail.

But God gives us hope.

Some plans succeed.
Some doors will close.
Some expectations go unmet.

But God gives us hope.

Dreams can be deferred.
Wishes may not come true.
Desires could go unfulfilled.

But God gives us hope.

Expectations can meet disappointment.
Prospects may not be realized.
Assumptions can be proven false.

But God gives us hope.

Predictions can be off base.
Assumptions may fall short.
Forecasting could miss the mark.

But God gives us hope.

***Scripture Reading: Romans 5:5***

# Personal Reflections

What does it mean to you when you read that "hope does not put us to shame"?

_____

_____

_____

_____

_____

_____

_____

What are your own "poetic reflections" and/or prayers to God that help you to hold on to hope when you are disappointed or discouraged?

_____

_____

_____

_____

_____

_____

_____

# To God

To the God of all.
To His one and only Son.

To our Savior and our King.
To the One Who hears every prayer.

To God Who sympathizes with our pain.
To our Lord Who knows our weaknesses.

To the One Who comforts and heals.
To Him Who has been both tempted and tested.

To God Who we can approach with confidence.
To our Savior Who we seek with reverence.

To the One Who has us in His mighty hands.
To Him Who paid it all for us.

To God Who we petition with confidence.
To our Savior we approach by faith.

To Him Who we can approach with boldness.
To our Redeemer Who paid the price for our sins.

To God Who gives us everlasting life.
To God Who gives us power and authority.

To God Who is the Lifter of our heads.
To God be the glory forevermore.

To God.

**Scripture Reading: Jude 24-25**

# Personal Reflections

This passage is called a "doxology," which means an expression of praise to God.[3] Write down your own doxology in honor of God.

_____

_____

_____

_____

_____

_____

_____

What are your own "poetic reflections" and/or prayers to God that can remind you to keep praising and thanking God?

_____

_____

_____

_____

_____

_____

_____

---

[3] https://www.oxfordreference.com/view/10.1093/oi/authority.20110803095729632

# All Things

All things.

Everything.

Total.

Entire.

Whole.

Complete.

Every little bit.

The works.

All-inclusive.

Whole ball of wax.

Whole enchilada.

Whole shebang.

Whole schmear.

Everything.

In all things,

God works!

***Scripture Reading: Romans 8:28***

# Personal Reflections

What are some "things," situations, or challenges that have taken place in your life that God worked out for your good?

_____

_____

_____

_____

_____

_____

_____

What are your own "poetic reflections" and/or prayers to God to remind you that in everything, He works for your good?

_____

_____

_____

_____

_____

_____

_____

# Just Because

A daily word.
Our sacred prayer.
A necessary act.
Our path toward healing.

For Who God is
In times of plenty;
For what God does
In times of trouble.

To heal our soul
With a grateful heart.
To mend our brokenness
With eyes fixed on God.

Just because of His mercy.
Just because of His grace.
Just because of His love.

Just because

He is God.

***Scripture Reading: Psalm 83:18***

# Personal Reflections

What are some ways in which you let others around you know that He is God in your life?

_____

_____

_____

_____

_____

_____

_____

What are your own "poetic reflections" and/or prayers to God to remind you that He alone is God and to praise Him—just because?

_____

_____

_____

_____

_____

_____

_____

# Launch Out

Listen to God.

For He is speaking.
For He is calling.
For He is directing.

Listen with God.

Seek out where it's deeper.
Launch out into the deepness.
Cast out into the deepest waters.

Listen for God.

Wait for a catch.
Watch for a harvest.
Get ready for an increase.

Listen.

Get ready.

To Launch Out.

***Scripture Reading: Luke 5:4***

# Personal Reflections

What are some of your personal fears that keep you from "launching out"?

_____

_____

_____

_____

_____

_____

_____

What are your own "poetic reflections" and/or prayers to God to encourage you to "launch out" with Him?

_____

_____

_____

_____

_____

_____

_____

_____

# A New Thing

Letting go of the old.
Forgetting that stuff in the past.
Taking hold of a new thing.

Leaving behind old matters.
Loosing that unnecessary baggage.
Grabbing onto a new thing.

Unleashing past hurts.
Releasing old grudges.
Embracing an unexpected new thing.

Detaching oneself from old ties.
Dismissing toxic people, places, and things.
Welcoming with joy a new thing.

Parting with old ways of thinking.
Abandoning old habits and patterns.
Leaning fully into a new thing.

Taking hold.
Grabbing onto.
Embracing strongly.
Welcoming with joy.
Leaning fully.

Into a new thing.

*Scripture Reading: Isaiah 43:18-19*

# Personal Reflections

What "new things" are you wanting God to do with you and for you during this season of your life? How can you be open to some "unexpected new things" that God may provide for you?

_____

_____

_____

_____

_____

_____

What are your own "poetic reflections" and/or prayers to God to help you not dwell on the past but look toward the future and some new opportunities?

_____

_____

_____

_____

_____

_____

_____

# My Heart's Desires

A pure heart—
Free from guilt,
Free from shame,
Free from hate,
Only by Your blood.

A clean heart—
Absent of anger,
Absent of fear,
Absent of unforgiveness,
Only by Your sacrifice.

A faithful heart—
Because of Your love,
Because of Your grace,
Because of Your mercy,
Only by Your stripes.

A loving heart—
Turned toward You,
Open for Your will,
Grateful for Your redemption,
Open to Your call.

***Scripture Reading: Psalm 51:10***

# Personal Reflections

What hopes, desires, or dreams are in your heart and spirit that need to be renewed or revived?

_____

_____

_____

_____

_____

_____

_____

What are your own "poetic reflections" and/or prayers to God to create in you a clean heart and renewed spirit?

_____

_____

_____

_____

_____

_____

_____

_____

# Daily Loveliness

Throughout each day,
Look for lovely things.
Take in lovely experiences.
Cherish lovely moments.
Make note of lovely acts.
Enjoy lovely views.
Await loveliness each day.

Within each day and every moment,
Share a lovely thought.
Give some lovely encouragement.
Proclaim a lovely truth.
Extend a lovely glance.
Offer a lovely word.
Expect loveliness each day.

In your walk,
Lift up lovely prayers.
Offer up lovely praise.
Speak a word of lovely confirmation.
Send up praise for lovely mercy.
Be grateful for lovely grace.
Receive lovely blessings each day.

***Scripture Reading: Philippians 4:8***

# Personal Reflections

What are some of the obstacles, fears, pains, or insecurities you think about that may block you from seeing whatever is lovely, admirable, or praiseworthy?

_____

_____

_____

_____

_____

_____

_____

_____

What are your own "poetic reflections" and/or prayers to God to help you better concentrate on "these things"?

_____

_____

_____

_____

_____

_____

_____

_____

# Highest Praise

For calling creation into being,
For creating the sun, stars, and moon,
For making the earth and everything in it,
I give You the highest praise.

For creating the birds of the air,
For providing food for all to eat,
For generating the land and the sea,
I give You the highest praise.

For making springs pour out water,
For making thunder roar at Your command,
For making winds subject to Your word,
I give You the highest praise.

For calling man and woman into being,
For calling each of us by name,
For calling the righteous to follow You,
I give You the highest praise.

To my Creator,
To my Sustainer,
To my Redeemer,
To my Provider,
To my Savior,

I give You the highest praise.

***Scripture Reading: Psalm 145: 1-3***

# Personal Reflections

In what ways do you offer God your "highest praise," and what situations or type of relationships might inhibit you from doing this?

_____

_____

_____

_____

_____

_____

_____

Write down your own "poetic reflections" and/or prayers to God as your commitment to giving Him your highest praise.

_____

_____

_____

_____

_____

_____

_____

# His Spirit

For God has given us His Spirit—
Not a spirit of fear,
Not a spirit of shame,
Not a spirit of regret.

For God has given us power
To call on His name,
To seek His face,
To lay our burdens down.

For God has given us love
That surpasses all understanding,
That is from everlasting to everlasting,
That this world cannot take away.

For God has given us a sound mind
So we can understand His Word,
So we can know the truth,
So we can remember what He's done.

***Scripture Reading: 2 Timothy 1:7***

# Personal Reflections

What problems, situations, or people cause you to experience fear, shame, or regret in your life?

_____

_____

_____

_____

_____

_____

_____

What are your own "poetic reflections" and/or prayers to God to remind you that He has not given us a spirit of fear?

_____

_____

_____

_____

_____

_____

_____

# Rejoice Always

Always rejoice
In good times,
In bad times,
In crazy times,
In uncertain times.

Give thanks
When things go well,
When things go wrong,
When you get your heart's desire,
When you don't.

Pray continually
For direction,
For comfort,
For clarity,
For purpose.

Commit yourself
To do His will,
To follow His lead,
To listen for His voice,
To praise His name.

*Scripture Reading: Philippians 4:4-7*

# Personal Reflections

What persistent thoughts or feelings create worry that keep you from being full of joy?

_____

_____

_____

_____

_____

_____

_____

What are your own "poetic reflections" and/or prayers to help you turn away from worry and focus on the promises of God that include joy?

_____

_____

_____

_____

_____

_____

_____

# About the Author

Audrey J. Murrell, Ph.D., is an author, elder, professor, and consultant. She grew up in Chicago, Illinois, where she was raised within the United Methodist church with her mother, father, two brothers, and one sister. Audrey left Chicago to study psychology at Howard University in Washington, D.C., where she earned a bachelor's degree and magna cum laude standing. After completing her undergraduate program, she continued her studies at the University of Delaware, where she earned both a masters and doctoral degree in psychology. Audrey found her way to Pittsburgh, Pennsylvania, where she joined the faculty at the University of Pittsburgh within the College of Business Administration. For three decades, she has been a professor, author, researcher, and consultant for many different organizations on topics such as mentoring, diversity, leadership, ethics, and social responsibility. As an author, she has published six books and over fifty professional articles. Dr. Murrell has received several recognitions, including the "Mayor's Citizen Service" award, which proclaimed August 12, "Dr. Audrey Murrell Day" within the city of Pittsburgh; *Pittsburgh Business Times's* "Woman of Influence" award; the "SBA Minority Business Champion of the Year" award; the University of Pittsburgh's "Student Choice" award; the "Women of Distinction" award from the Girl Scouts of Southwestern Pennsylvania; the Susan B. Anthony "Women of Vision" award; the "Community Champion" award from the United Way of Allegheny County; the Shyne Foundation's Gwendolyn Elliot "Lifetime

Achievement" award; and the "Woman of the Year" award by Onyx Women's Network and Magazine. Audrey continues to follow God's calling within her work in the church, across the campus, and within the community. She resides in Pittsburgh, Pennsylvania, where she is an active member and an ordained elder at Bidwell Street United Presbyterian Church, affectionately known as "The Well."

www.ingramcontent.com/pod-product-compliance
Ingram Content Group UK Ltd.
Pitfield, Milton Keynes, MK11 3LW, UK
UKHW041944230426
12048UKWH00008B/127